"Seeds"

Published by Evolu-Sol Publishing

First Edition 2012

Illustrations by Isella Vega

"Seeds"

"Seeds"

For my brothers and sisters, cousins,

nieces, nephews and neighbours all around the world...

with love

"Seeds"

'SEEDS'

By

David Ankrah

"Seeds"

There once was a very happy land with very happy people called Zoniye. The Zoniye people cared for each other, helped each other, and showed respect for each other in every way, for as long as anyone can remember. It was as if they were just one big happy family.

Life was good, and they all worked together to make sure there was always enough food to go around. No one ever pushed or shoved, no one seemed to get angry, and no one ever tried to take anything from anyone else.

In Zoniye, whenever a man and woman fell in love, everyone got together and helped to build a strong new home made out of materials from the earth and the woods. Every time this happened it was such a joyous occasion and there would be a great celebration, with everyone singing and laughing while they were working. The people of Zoniye made sure that the man and woman had everything they needed to bring up their children in happy, peaceful, and loving surroundings. It was simply part of the Zoniye way of life. 'Care for others as you would your own. Respect the fact that you are alive. Let your love for life guide your actions. Never make anyone's life difficult in any way.'

For several generations there was harmony, and a wonderful peace in Zoniye. Each and every day was a blessing.

Then one unfortunate day, some dark and mysterious outsiders came into Zoniye on strange machines. They seemed friendly enough at first, but then slowly, they began to convince the Zoniye people that things could be even better if a few things changed. The mysterious outsiders wanted to bring in some new rules. They wanted to wear down the spirit of the Zoniye people, and devised a big plan to make sure all of the people of Zoniye forgot about who they were and how they used to live.

The ruler of the dark and mysterious outsiders was called Nastalior, and he sent all his servants out to all parts of Zoniye, to convince all the Zoniye people to do work for him. Nastalior taught his servants clever ways in which they could control the Zoniye people, with carefully chosen words and promises, and also with seeds..., seeds which the Zoniye people could only get after doing some work set by Nastalior's servants. Nastalior also made his servants put up barricades and fences around most of the land so now the only way that the Zoniye people could feed themselves... was with seeds.

Very soon, the whole land had changed, and many of the dreams that the Zoniye people once had were forgotten. They would work nearly everyday from the time the sun rose into the beautiful Zoniye sky, right the way through until the sun disappeared behind the mountains. As the days and months went by, more and more Zoniye people were realising that they were not nearly as happy as they once were...

"Seeds"

One of the Zoniye people, called Palooko, still held on to the memory of how his people used to be. He dreamt of the day when they could be that way once more. Happy, caring, joyous and loving. He knew that it could take a very long time before things changed, but he remained faithful, believing that if he worked smart enough and inspired others, his dream could one day come true.

Another one of the Zoniye people, called Greecho, had completely accepted the new way of life shown by the dark and mysterious outsiders. He hadn't completely forgotten about the way that the Zoniye people used to be, but he now had absolutely no interest in going back to helping others in the way that they used to. He was more concerned with the seeds he was getting everyday.

The days were long and hard, and as time went on, the Zoniye people became more and more unhappy just doing the work set by Nastalior's servants, but they needed seeds..., it was the only way they could feed themselves, so there was not much else they could do...

Everyday, after collecting his seeds from Nastalior's servants, Greecho would go home and use all his seeds to make soups and pies and fill his belly full.

Palooko, on the other hand, would take his seeds home to his family, and then he would split the seeds into three piles. He gave one pile to his wonderful wife and she would lovingly make delicious meals for them to enjoy. The second pile would go into their seed cupboard for another day, and he put the third pile into a special jar. Palooko had special plans for this special jar.

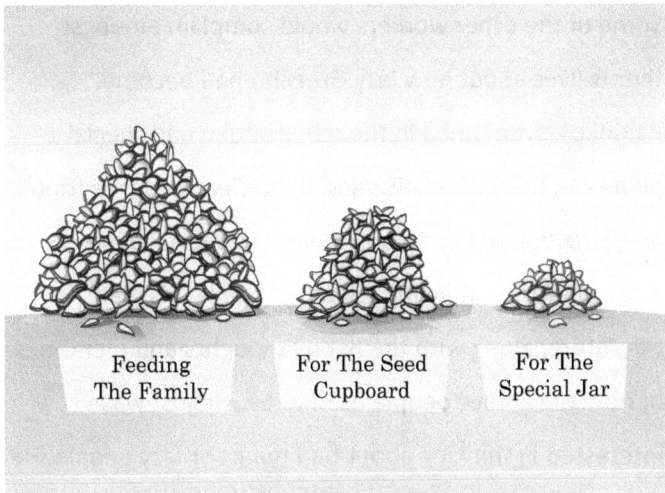

| Feeding The Family | For The Seed Cupboard | For The Special Jar |

Palooko always split his seeds into three piles...

"Seeds"

Many moons went by and the Zoniye people did much work. Nastalior's servants would notice that on some tasks, some of the Zoniye people did more of the work than others, and even though they saw these differences, they would still give all of them the same amount of seeds everyday.

Greecho was one of the lazier workers and he always seemed to get away with not doing too much work. As long as he got his seeds at the end of each day he didn't care.

Some of the other workers would complain amongst themselves about how lazy Greecho had become. Palooko never joined in though. Palooko had special plans and he wanted his mind to be clear and free from anything that didn't help him with his special plans. He much preferred thinking about his family, his plans for the future, along with the happy thoughts and memories of how the Zoniye people used to be. He just wasn't interested in thinking about bad things or lazy people. He didn't want to waste his valuable time, his mind, or his energy in that way. He didn't think he was cleverer than

anyone else, he just felt that everyone's mind was truly
amazing and designed to think about much better
things...

After some time, when Palooko's special jar was just over
three quarters full with seeds, he decided that it was
time to begin the next part of his special plan. He told his
wife and children that he loved them, he always wanted
the very best for them, and he wanted them to always
have enough seeds.

Palooko had heard tale of how you can makes seeds
grow, but only if you put enough seeds in the right place
at the right time. He told his wife and children that he
would start looking for these places, and that he might
not find the right place straight away, but he would keep
looking and keep trying until he found somewhere that
would make their seeds grow. He told his family that he
might lose some seeds along the way, but he would only
use seeds from the special jar. That was also the reason
why he always put some seeds into the seed cupboard,

so that if he wanted to, he could even take time away from doing the work for Nastalior to look for these places, and his family would still be able to eat.

Another reason he always put some seeds in the seed cupboard was because he noticed that, for some unknown reason, sometimes Nastalior's servants didn't look very well. Sometimes they wouldn't be able to move properly for days, and the same thing had started happening to some of the Zoniye people too. Palooko didn't want his family to go without seeds if *he* couldn't get up to go and work.

Word spread to many of the great lands far away, about how popular seeds had become in Zoniye, and even more new outsiders came from afar. Seeds had become the most important thing to just about everyone who lived in Zoniye, and it wasn't long before many of the Zoniye people began to complain about not having enough seeds. They often thought they were doing too much work for the amount of seeds they were getting.

It wasn't long before several new outsiders had moved into Zoniye, becoming friends with Nastalior. Some of these new outsiders brought new creations with them that the Zoniye people had never seen before, and they would show them off at every opportunity. The Zoniye people got very curious indeed and they wanted to find out how they could have some of these new creations. The outsiders said it was very simple. They would exchange their new creations for some seeds...

And so, many of the Zoniye people began to exchange seeds for these new, exciting creations. The new outsiders really liked seeds and they liked the idea of getting seeds this way so they began to bring more new creations and big fancy shiny things to Zoniye. They would parade them through the streets and everyone looked with admiration. Some of the females of Zoniye became so interested in the big fancy shiny things that they even started to ignore some of the male Zoniye people, if they didn't have, or couldn't give them, any of the fancy shiny things...men and women in Zoniye weren't falling in love as much as they used to...

"Seeds"

Greecho would often see the new outsiders with their new creations and he knew that he couldn't have any of them because he would need to give the outsiders a LOT of seeds, which he didn't have. It was much, much more than what he was getting for his work. This often made him a sad and grumpy.

Don't forget, Greecho always liked to use all of his seeds to make soups and pies to fill his belly full.

One group of seed loving new outsiders had a new idea. They started to stand on the corners of the streets and tempt the Zoniye people with big bags of seeds. The idea was that if they wanted to have a lot of seeds now, they could borrow some of the big bags, then all they had to do was promise to give the new outsiders a portion of the seeds they got from their work on a regular basis. And they would have to promise to do this for several suns and several moons.

This sounded quite good to the Zoniye people who didn't have enough seeds to exchange for some of the big fancy shiny things... and so many of them couldn't resist taking up the offer.

Time went on and many of the Zoniye people became sadder and sadder. They started to realise that the amount of seeds they had promised to give to the new outsiders was going to be way too much, but they couldn't go back on their promise. They had promised to give the new outsiders a portion of their seeds, for many suns and many moons, and all in return for borrowing those big bags of seeds. At the same time they still saw and still wanted even more of the new creations and big fancy shiny things...

By now the Zoniye people had completely forgotten that they were once a happy people, who helped each other in so many ways, making sure that everyone had all that they needed. Above all they had respect for each other, and they use to laugh, sing, dance and tell stories everyday.

But now, some of the Zoniye people were so desperate to get their hands on the big fancy shiny things, that they even started to try and steal seeds from other Zoniye people! One group of Zoniye people even got together to make fake seeds and tried to use them as real seeds.

Nastalior found out about the fake seeds, and he gave the order that the guilty makers of fake seeds should be chained up, made an example of, and then locked in a cave underneath the wasteland outside Zoniye.

Palooko did his best to avoid the new outsiders with all their new creations and big fancy shiny things. Even though he liked some of the things he saw, he knew that they wanted a lot of seeds for them, and he wanted to carry out his special plans first. He was still thinking about what a lot of Zoniye people didn't know, believe or realise. Seeds can make more seeds ... If you have enough, and you put your seeds in the right places at the right time, seeds can grow and you will end up with even more seeds than before. So everyday, after working for Nastalior's servants, Palooko went in search of good places to put the seeds that he was collecting in his special jar.

Greecho had become very miserable, and he often lost his temper quickly with some of the Zoniye people over the simplest of things. But he always had a very big smile for Nastalior's servants and any of the other outsiders. He hoped that he might be able to get extra seeds from them.

Because Greecho had always used all of his seeds to make soups and stews, and eat them all on the same day, he had asked the new outsiders for some of their big bags of seeds, promising to give them a portion the seeds that he got from his daily work for several moons.

In fact, Greecho had asked for big bags of seeds on more than one occasion, which meant he was actually giving more and more seeds back to the new outsiders at each new moon. What he hadn't yet realised, is that he would end up giving the new outsiders far more seeds than the amount of seeds he had borrowed in the first place.

Because he was giving such a large amount of his seeds to the new outsiders, Greecho was not able to make the same amount of soups and pies anymore. This made

Greecho even grumpier. A couple of times, Greecho even tried to hide from the new outsiders to try and keep the seeds to himself. The new outsiders were very unhappy when they found out and so they came to Greecho's home and took some of his possessions. They also made him give back even *more* seeds at the next new moon to make up for it.

Meanwhile, Palooko was still searching for a good place to make his seeds grow. He had tried to grow his seeds a few times already but with no luck. Some of the Zoniye people thought he was crazy. They would tell him he wasting good seeds on a fairytale. But those same people didn't really have a lot of seeds themselves anyway. They would often complain about their lack of seeds, and end up doing almost the same thing that Greecho was doing, asking for big bags of seeds because they used up nearly all of their seeds all of the time.

Palooko was happy that he had always split his seeds into the three piles, because on top of everything else, he was now able to help some of the older Zoniye people who could no longer work as much for Nastalior's servants. He would sometimes give them some of the seeds he had kept in his cupboard. Palooko was especially happy that his wife encouraged him to keep searching for places to make the seeds grow. He loved that she was so supportive, and it made him love her even more.

Most people would have given up after losing even a small amount of seeds, but Palooko believed that he would one day find the right place...and he was right.

Many of Nastalior's servants knew good places to make seeds grow but they didn't really want to share what they knew with the people of Zoniye.

The next day, after work, Palooko went to a new place he had discovered not too far from where some of Nastalior's servants stayed. He put his seeds in place.

Three years later, Greecho was still working hard. In fact, he was working even harder than before, and he was still giving the new outsiders a share of the seeds he received for his work. He was even asking Nastalior's servants if he could continue working after the sun went behind the mountains to try and get more seeds from them.

You see…he couldn't get any more big bags of seeds from the new outsiders. Not too long ago, Greecho had the same sickness that some of Nastalior's servants had, which meant he couldn't go to work. And that meant that he didn't have enough seeds to feed himself. Which also meant that he couldn't give a portion of his seeds back to the outsiders as he had promised. They didn't trust him anymore. They didn't care that he was sick. They just wanted their seeds.

Palooko, on the other hand, didn't have to work everyday anymore. He was so happy because he could spend much more time with his wife and children. The new outsiders would always ask him if he wanted any big bags of seeds, but Palooko didn't need any. You see….the seeds that Palooko had put in place three years ago was now a glorious tree with many branches, and on each of the branches were pods, and inside each of these pods you would find some… seeds. And even though this tree was giving Palooko and his family more seeds than they

needed, they still split all of the seeds into three piles:
The first pile was for feeding the family, the second pile
was put into the seed cupboard, and the third pile was
put into one of his special jars...as you now know Palooko
has special plans for the seeds in the special jars.

Palooko could also spend more time talking to other
Zoniye people, and slowly reminding them of how they
used to care for and help one another. He told them
about his dream that one day they would be able to have
fields of these trees that made seeds, and that everyone
would love, respect and help each other in the happy and
harmonious way that the Zoniye people used to be. A lot
of the Zoniye people started to love the idea and agreed
to help in anyway they could. They could see how it
meant that their children would have happier lives in the
future.

Of course, at first, Greecho didn't want to help...but
when he started to see how happy and excited the
Zoniye people started to become, he felt left out. In fact
he realised that even if he did want to help, he
couldn't...especially if he continued doing what he was

doing. Working after the sun went behind the mountains didn't seem to be helping very much. He still used whatever seeds he had left everyday on soups and pies. He was so used to doing what he was doing that he was actually afraid of changing and doing something new. He knew he had to change, but ... he felt stuck in his ways.

What would you do if you were Greecho?...Do you think you could change?

Meanwhile, Palooko continued to encourage the Zoniye people to look for good places for their own seeds, and as the years went on many of the Zoniye people didn't have to work for Nastalior's and his servants for all of their lives anymore.

Sadly, Greecho seemed to have no choice but to keep working...until of course the day he either passed away or decided to have real faith in the true Zoniye way of life, start helping others, and use his seeds in a much better way.

So, who would you like to have been?

Palooko – Happy, Helping, Loving, Inspiring

Greecho – Sad, Selfish, Grumpy, Worn Out

Interesting how their lives turned out isn't it? And guess what?

They both started... with the **same** amount of seeds...

So whenever you come across some seeds... maybe you will remember this story... and think to yourself...Would I like to be like Palooko? Or would I want to be like Greecho?... You have the choice...you decide...

"Seeds"

"Seeds"

"Seeds"

Afterword

Before Nastalior and his servants came into Zoniye, I think I would have liked to have been a part of their community.

It seems as though they lived life simply and with joy, love and respect for one another.

The introduction of seeds in Zoniye could be seen as a good thing or a bad thing. However, Palooko and Greecho had two completely different stories, even though they were getting the same amount of seeds.

How is your story looking at the moment?...

If you're wondering what I mean...go back and read the story again, but this time whenever you see the word 'seeds' replace it with the word on the next page...

"Seeds"

Money

Thank you for reading

"Seeds"

Everything good starts with the mind

Why waste your mind's time thinking about things that

make you unhappy?

www.liveinpositivity.com

www.seedsthechildrensbook.com

Other books by David Ankrah

"Don't Do What I Did" - 10 Ways To Avoid Some Of The Common Traps And Mistakes When It Comes To Personal Money Matters

"Seeds"

"Seeds"